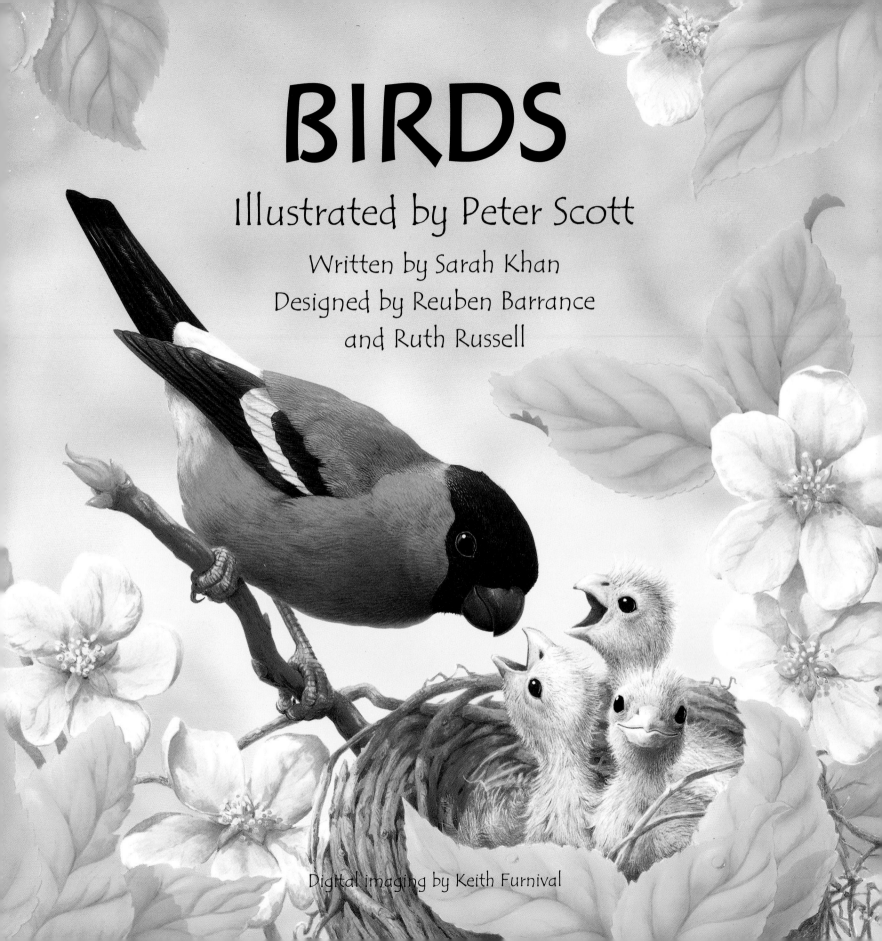

BIRDS

Illustrated by Peter Scott

Written by Sarah Khan

Designed by Reuben Barrance
and Ruth Russell

Digital imaging by Keith Furnival

Hummingbirds

Hummingbirds are the tiniest birds in the world. They drink nectar, a sugary food made by flowers.

What's this bird doing?

This bird is as small as a butterfly.

He flaps his wings so quickly that they make a humming sound.

The bird's feet are so small that she can't walk or hop and has to fly everywhere.

Hummingbirds build nests out of twigs, moss and spiders' webs.

Flamingos

Flamingos eat tiny water animals and plants. This is what makes their feathers pink.

She turns her head upside down in the water to find food.

A flamingo has long legs so it can stand in water without getting its feathers wet.

She uses her beak like a strainer.

Ssslurp!

Lots of flamingos live together like a very big family.

This flamingo is standing on one leg. His other leg is folded up close to his body.

Here's a baby hatching out of its shell. He needs some help.

Get me out!

Birds of paradise

Male birds of paradise have fancy feathers. They show off to make female birds look at them.

This bird is showing off to someone. Can you find her?

He lifts his tail and spreads his wings. He looks amazing.

"Paradise" means heaven. These birds got their name because they looked like they came from heaven.

Lift the flap to see this bird make himself even more beautiful.

Eagles

Eagles hunt small animals for food. As they fly through the air, they look for food on the ground.

This eagle has seen something moving in the bush. She swoops down to catch it.

What has the eagle seen?

This is a golden eagle. She has golden feathers on her head.

This is a bald eagle. He isn't really bald, but he looks bald because his head is white.

He is carrying a fish home to his chicks.

Parrots

Parrots live in hot, rainy forests. Their feathers are very bright and shiny.

They have strong beaks that are good for cracking nuts.

This parrot is hungry. Lift the flap to see him eat.

Forests can be dangerous places for birds. Can you see what has frightened this parrot away?

Squawk!
Look out!

The parrot squawks to warn other parrots of danger.

Finches

In the spring, finches build nests in trees and bushes.

These will look great in my nest.

This bird has found some twigs to build her nest with.

This bird is too busy collecting food to help build the nest. What has he seen under the leaf?

Here is a mother bird in her nest. She is waiting for the father bird to bring her some food.

Open the nest to see inside.

Penguins

Penguins can't fly and are not good runners. They are best at swimming.

The birds on these pages are called little blue penguins. They are the smallest of all penguins.

The penguin's feet are like flippers. They help him to steer. His wings help him to swim.

Look out, fishes, the penguin is going to eat you!

After a tiring day at sea, this penguin comes back to the land to sleep.

He jumps onto the rocks.

Penguins can only waddle on land. This is because their legs are very short.

This book has shown you some of the
amazing birds that live around the world.
But it would take thousands of books
like this to show them all...

Edited by Judy Tatchell

Published in 2004 by Usborne Publishing Ltd, Usborne House, 83-85 Saffron Hill, London EC1N 8RT, England.
www.usborne.com
Copyright © Usborne Publishing Ltd, 2004.